A Woman Worthy

Aisha Arcangel

BookLeaf Publishing

India | USA | UK

Presentation by *BookLeaf Publishing*

Web: www.bookleafpub.com

E-mail: info@bookleafpub.com

ISBN: 9789360946012

First edition 2024

For my younger self - have faith, beautiful girl. Your light burns so bright, no one will ever snuff it out.

ACKNOWLEDGEMENT

To my love, J.B - thank you for your unwavering support in all my endeavors. You make life beautiful and I'm glad I get to spend it with you. I love you.

To my loved ones who have gone from this earth - thank you for spending our years together loving me unconditionally.

To my closest friends - thank you for believing in me, even when I couldn't.

To my former lovers - thank you for your many lessons; I will never forget them.

Thank you, Jesus, for the life I have. You make all things possible.

PREFACE

Dearest Reader,

The following poems have been written and re-written over the course of a very difficult decade of my life; my 20s were not "the best days of my life," as those before my time had led me to believe. In fact, I struggled. A lot. I struggled with the notion that I was worthy of love. I struggled with the more ridiculous idea that I had any sort of talent, or that my puny life had any significance at all. It was unfathomable to me that anything I could create would make its way out into the world and see any sort of success, so I simply never tried. I spent so much time measuring myself up to the accomplishments of others that I remained paralyzed from fear of failure; incessant "what ifs" loomed over me and kept me so small and afraid that I never realized what a gift my life and talents were, that it would not matter if I failed – so long as I tried. I want to tell you, Dearest Reader, that having the right people in your corner makes a world of difference – it did for me. So here I am, facing what is quite possibly my biggest fear, and here you are, holding in your hands my most prized accomplishment to date. Handle it with care.

With all my affection,
Aisha

Imposter

A record of victories
and accolades line
my walls;
all bear my name,
none belong to me.

Old Musings

While tossing the old
to give way for the new,
I found a thought
written down,
stashed away,
and long forgotten:

"As elusive as you are,
I can only hope
to catch you,
to have you in my arms,
on my lips,
and in my bed."

The memory of whoever
you are must be
buried deep,
deep down
much like this note,
to be uncovered
years after
the ink
of my feelings
have faded.

Love Letter to My Inner Child

Somewhere and everywhere
right this very second,
there is a little brown girl
looking at herself in the mirror
and declaring herself
 "ugly."

What she does not know
is that every cell in her body
is a wonder, a miracle, a masterpiece.

I think of the little brown girl that lives in me,
and I remember

her dark brown curls, perfect spirals atop her
head
her skin, the color of cafe con leche
her dark brown eyes, bright and sparkling and
full of imagination

and how she would beat herself bloody
with ugly words forcefully thrust into her hands
by ugly people envious of her glow.

I say to her:

Little girl,
every cell in your body
is a wonder, a miracle, a masterpiece.

You are beautiful.

Naked Humor

"You're tiny," you say
as you wrap your fingers
around my much smaller ones
to crack my knuckles,
one by one.

No one's ever done that before.

"I am tiny," I whisper,
as I sit up
to look at you in the dim light
of my equally
tiny
studio apartment.
Your hazel eyes
meet my dark browns,
your crooked smile poised in a smirk.

Something in your expression
challenges me not to laugh,
but I cannot help it.

I bury my head
into your curly-haired chest,
red from hours in the sun,

our naked bodies trembling
as we giggle uncontrollably.

Your calloused hands
caress my bare skin
ever so softly and
I wonder
how a giant could be so gentle.

Not The Same

Against my will,
I keep tiny pieces
of the men who have left me
in my memory.

Every time I crack a smile, I recall
how one lover pointed out
that the left side of my mouth
raises faster than
the right side.
A beautiful
lopsided
grin.

I wonder how long
it took him to notice.
Before him,
my involuntary quirk
hadn't even occurred to me.
I tried to change it,
tried to control the uncontrollable,
just so I could say
"I'm not the same."

Though I can't recall

the sound of your voice when
you'd speak my name through
your smirking lips,
I can still feel your warm hands
grasping mine to crack my knuckles.

I've tried to kick the habit,
tried to keep from applying pressure
on my fingers
to simulate the feel of your hands
on mine, to no avail.

I want so badly to erase the memory,
so when you come back -
because men like you
always, always come back -
I can say,
"I'm not the same."

Santa Muerte

I was a child
when I first met Santa Muerte.
She cradled my mother in her arms
and we locked eyes.
"I'll be back for you some day."
That was over twenty years ago.
Death comes for us all,
but unlike most, I don't wish
to wait for her.
There's a longing in my bones
to see my mother again,
a deeper longing
to greet Santa Muerte as an old friend.
But every time I try to surprise her
she sends me away.
She says, gazing upon me lovingly,
"Not today."

Our Fingertips Dripped Red

I remember what you called it - "una manzana
china"-
as you opened up the fruit and revealed the
glistening seeds you were about to eat.
"Ven, pruebelo," you beckoned, as you offered
me
a piece of the mystery fruit to try.
Your gap-toothed smile was wide,
and your fingertips dripped red.

Pom-e-gra-nate. Pomegranate.
I hadn't learned the name until I was a few years
older.
But I was quickly acquainted with the fruit's
exotic sweetness and I would often be found
affixed to a seat at your glass dining room table,
plucking rubies and garnets from its flesh and
relishing the tiny explosions of
sweet pomegranate juice.

You enjoyed expanding my palate in the hopes
that
I might be an adventurous woman like you, and
so
we would often sit together,

picking apart the bejeweled fruit and enjoying
the sweetness of its seeds.

In these instances of my youth, time seemed to
stand still.
Now a woman grown, I sit alone
in my tiny apartment with a pomegranate
cracked open
on my kitchen counter,
and I imagine that each
succulent
morsel
that I savor
is a moment that I steal back from time.

In those stolen moments, we are together again,
our fingertips dripping red.

Lindos Recuerdos

Do you remember when we ran out of flour
during our attempt to make pastelillos?
Our fingers sticky from the dough,
tears of laughter streaming down our
scrunched-up faces,
we formed the meat-filled pastries.
They tasted like home;
no other pastelillo has tasted the same to me
since.

Remember how being away from you
would send me into an inconsolable tantrum?
You were my favorite person and I was your
muñeca.
You'd made me a dollhouse
out of scraps of cardboard and fabric and pure,
pure love.
It was my favorite thing to play with
whenever I would spend nights at your house,
where I'd lie awake at night,
listening to your soft voice, praying

Dios te salve, Maria
Llena eres de gracia

echoing through the wall as if
you were pleading at Our Lady's very feet.
Did you know that I'd hear your voice
resounding in my head many years later
while holding the very same beads you'd used to
pray?
I keep them with me at all times,
and as I kneel and pray for you,
I hold them - and you - close to my heart.

Coin Toss

I remember the first time I'd watched a coin toss.
My abuela balanced a quarter on her
wide nail bed, flicked it as though giving
a quick thumbs-up to the heavens,
and with a deft, heavy hand
caught and smacked the coin
down onto the back of her spotted, wrinkled
palm.

"Cabezas," she called. Her hand moved away,
revealing Washington's face. Heads, indeed.

I don't believe we'd made a bet; this was just for
fun.
Another silent lesson, as Abuela's lessons often
were.
Her hands,
though weathered and weakened with age,
were magic to me.
I'd press her soft, plush fingertips and every
tiny squeeze briefly offered bunches of red rose
petals
before returning to flesh.

There are days I miss her terribly,

though she's been gone for what seems like a
lifetime.
There are days when life feels too heavy to
carry,
too heavy to trudge through.
On those days, I toss a coin.

'Heads, I stay. Tails, I join you, Abuela.'

It always lands on Heads.

Immobile

All it takes is one shaky landing
to send you crashing down, along with
all of your weighty ambition.
Body frozen, mind racing,
plans set months ago never fulfilled.
There you sit, suffocated
by the uncertainty of your future.
Wanting to move forward,
unable to see past the nebulae
in your crystal ball, you sit immobile
and wait for clarity.

The Big Breakup

Nearly seven years together we spent.
At first so happy and compliant, I became
jaded by your constant demands.

First you wanted my time - I freely gave it.
Then you wanted my sanity - I could feel you
forcefully tugging at it,
my iron grip turning to putty with every pull.
Was it the so-called stability that kept me loyal?
Or was it that you choked the life
out of every heartfelt hope and lofty dream I
had?

I left before I could gather all my things,
before the nosy neighbors could peek
from their windows and cast their
judgmental glances, before they could
learn the truth:
that I, in all my stubbornness,
refused to leave you first.
That you, from the pedestal I'd foolishly put you
on,
had forced me out.

They'd all know soon enough anyway.

I sat catatonic, sobs choking me,
my vision blurry from bitter tears.
Suddenly,
as though I'd been struck by lightning,
I realized:

by casting me out,
you'd given me my freedom.

Hungover

Like a glass of sweet Southern moonshine,
your lips meet mine over and over; a delicious
danger so easily imbibed.
Filled with the kind of courage one finds at
the bottom of a bottle, our hands explore
each other's bodies - you search for the sweet
spots carefully hidden under the layers of my
sundress and personal baggage and I,
with all my inhibitions put to rest, glide my free
hand
to your favorite place, listening for your moans.
Two become one, but only for what seems to be
a short moment; summer's time runs out
like sand in a sieve.
The sun comes up on our nakedness and we
exchange awkward glances, covering
ourselves as if standing in the middle of Eden,
awash with shame.
We part ways,
silently wearing to ourselves
to never
drink of each other
again.

Inundated

I set the intention:
"I will do the thing!"
Then the day comes
and the doubts
begin to pour in
through the cracks
in the hull of my ship,
where I sink below my blankets,
enveloped in warmth and worry.

Silver

21

With a fine-toothed comb
I draw an even line,
separating waves of dark chocolate brown
upon my curly crown.
Encountering a patch of wiry strands
in shades of gray and catching glints of silver,
I begin to count all the ways life
has stolen my youth

Twenty-Eight

I opened my eyes
and took a breath
to remind myself of those
who won't wake up
ever again.
"This storm will pass,"
I say to myself, even though
it feels like a bold lie.
Still, I press on,
grateful
for the chance
to keep on living.

The Struggle.

I thought I knew what I wanted to say.
But my thoughts, as always,
are a muddled mess.
So I started over.
And over.
And over again.
My wastebasket full
of scraps.
The words you see
on this page
are not the words
I'd scribbled down
in what I perceived to be
a moment of brilliance.
My bulb is dim.
No spark remains.
I'll try again later.

Alleluia

On my knees
I,
a sinner of the worst kind
come to praise You
in all
Your Mercy
and all
Your Love -
the love you show me,
a sinner of the worst kind.

Even when I place You
in the furthest reaches of my scattered mind,
I open my eyes and there You are
all around me, holding me close.

Alleluia,
  Alleluia,
    Alleluia

I sing, my bruised heart full and beating.
Your presence brings me life.

I pray You never leave.

Thirty-One

On the eve of my 31st birthday,
I discovered new patches of dreaded silver
hair, barely grown in.
They'd begun to sprout like stubborn weeds,
hidden amongst healthy bulbs and saplings.
I slowly pulled them from the fertile ground
on my crown, satisfying yet futile attempt
to undo the natural consequences of time.
While combing through dark brown tresses
to search for pesky grays and silvers,
I was reminded of all the years I would have
wasted
if I'd had my way;
instead of gray hairs, my skull would be
riddled with worms and covered in dust and dirt.

But God's will is greater.

Suddenly aware of the tremendous gift
I'd been given, I set the tweezers aside.

I think I'll keep the gray.

Lovely

I wake up some mornings
in awe of my body.
My freshly-shaven legs rub against each other;
just outside my window
a cricket chirps in time
with the friction of my smooth skin
against my clean bedsheets.
My hands slowly make their way down to my
waist,
made plush over the years, and rest on my soft
belly.
My fingertips lightly trace
a long, hair-thin scar - a subtle reminder
that six year-olds shouldn't play
in cardboard boxes.
My palms lightly cup my chin and caress
my full cheeks;
I can feel the efforts of my daily routine - almost
no blemishes remain.
I run my fingers through my tousled hair,
making note of how my curls
spiral gently downward, and smile to myself.

Sunrises & Rooftops

27

Elevator to the fifth floor of a quiet building
Leads to a rooftop overlooking the parts of
Brooklyn so often ignored by passersby
But here we are watching it all unfold
As the the sky turns its dark blues into indigos
Pinks and siennas and the sun peeks out
From what seems to be a rip in the Universe
Here we are watching it all unfold drinking in
Pure beauty and serenity before we drift back
Into our busy lives and dream of tonight
forever

Holy Hour

A man stands before me.
Brown skin, shoulder length brown hair
and eyes dark and bold,
like my cup of coffee before
I've diluted it with sugar-sweet milk.

I know Him.

I kneel at His wounded feet and with tears in my
eyes,
recount my latest failures.
He smiles, lowering Himself to sit
cross-legged, facing me.
He pauses to light a cigarette;
I see the smoke rising through the holes in His
hands
as He takes a long drag.
He ponders my weighty confession,
and exhales smoke from the corner of His
mouth.
"My beloved daughter," He says, flicking ashes
into an ashtray
of His own making,
"I forgive you. And I love you."

The smoke smells not of tobacco, but of sweet
frankincense.
We sit in silence for a brief moment;
I bask in His presence.
He ashes His half-smoked cigarette and
extinguishes it
on His knee before getting up.
He kisses my forehead,
lifts my chin so that my eyes meet His and
whispers,
"I'll see you on Sunday."

He walks away, pocketing the remnant of His
cigarette,
His saggy jeans dragging on the ground beneath
His sandals.

I feel saved.

www.ingramcontent.com/pod-product-compliance
Lightning Source LLC
La Vergne TN
LVHW010838200726
843508LV00012B/2645